BIRTHDAYS!

A KEEPSAKE MEMORY BOOK
TO CELEBRATE EACH YEAR

RUBY OAKS

Castle Point Books
New York

www.stmartins.com
www.castlepointbooks.com

The Castle Point Books trademark is owned by Castle Point Publications, LLC.
Castle Point books are published and distributed by St. Martin's Press.

ISBN 978-1-250-22853-6 (hardcover)

Design by Tara Long
Composition by Noora Cox

Images used under license from Shutterstock.com

Our books may be purchased in bulk for promotional, educational, or business use. Please
contact your local bookseller or the Macmillan Corporate and Premium Sales Department
at 1-800-221-7945, extension 5442, or by email at MacmillanSpecialMarkets@macmillan.com.

First Edition: September 2019

10 9 8 7 6 5 4 3 2 1

INTRODUCTION

THIS BOOK IS FOR YOU, ..., BECAUSE

I WANT YOU TO KNOW ....

....

EACH TIME YOU BLOW OUT ANOTHER CANDLE, REMEMBER THAT I

....

....

OVER THE YEARS, I HOPE ....

.... MAY EACH BIRTHDAY BRING YOU ....,

................................., AND ...., MY ....!

LOVE, ...

WONDERFUL AT 1

LENGTH AT BIRTH

....

HEIGHT AT AGE 1

....

LOOK HOW MUCH YOU'VE GROWN FROM THE DAY YOU CAME INTO THE WORLD TO YOUR FIRST BIRTHDAY!

NEW DISCOVERIES THIS YEAR

YOUR FIRST FRIENDS

....

....

....

....

....

....

ALL YOU CAN DO

....

....

....

....

....

1

GETTING TO KNOW YOU

YOU MAKE EVERYONE LAUGH WHEN ....

YOU GET FRUSTRATED WHEN ....

AT THIS AGE, YOU LOOK VERY MUCH LIKE

....

↓

📷

YEARS FROM NOW, I CAN IMAGINE YOU

....

WHAT MAKES YOU SMILE

ACTIVITIES ....

....

....

TOYS ....

....

FOOD ....

....

PEOPLE ....

....

PLACES ....

....

BOOKS ....

....

MUSIC ....

....

1

BIRTHDAY FUN

WE CELEBRATED YOUR FIRST BIRTHDAY WITH

THEME ....

GUESTS ....

ACTIVITIES ....

THE HIGHLIGHT OF THE CELEBRATION WAS

....

CELEBRATING YOU

THIS PHOTO TOTALLY CAPTURES YOU BEING YOU!

THREE WORDS
THAT DESCRIBE YOU

....

....

....

FROM ME TO YOU...

CHECK THE
BACK POCKET

1

TERRIFIC AT 2

SO MUCH IS NEW AT 2! HERE ARE A FEW DISCOVERIES
YOU'VE MADE OR SKILLS YOU'VE MASTERED THIS YEAR.

TODDLER TALK

THE AFFECTIONATE NICKNAMES WE CALL YOU

....

....

WHAT YOU CALL YOUR FAVORITE PEOPLE AND THINGS

....

....

HOW WE SHOW OUR LOVE
FOR EACH OTHER

....

....

....

....

....

....

2

A DAY IN YOUR LIFE

WE START THE DAY BY

....

OUR BEDTIME ROUTINE
INCLUDES

....

....

....

....

SHHH!
YOU'RE SLEEPING

YOUR FAVORITE TIME OF THE DAY IS .... AM / PM

THAT'S WHEN YOU

....

THIS IS YOU

TOY YOU PLAY WITH THE MOST ....
....

SONG YOU'RE MOST LIKELY TO BE SINGING ....
....

BOOK YOU ASK TO READ OVER AND OVER ....
....

WHAT YOU LOVE TO WEAR ....
....

FOODS YOU FUSS ABOUT ....
....

HOW YOU MAKE ME LAUGH ....
....

HOW I MAKE YOU LAUGH ....
....

2

BIRTHDAY FUN

WE CELEBRATED YOUR SECOND BIRTHDAY WITH

THEME ....

GUESTS ....

ACTIVITIES ....

THE HIGHLIGHT OF THE CELEBRATION WAS

....

TOGETHER TIME

ONE OF MY FAVORITE MEMORIES FROM THE PAST YEAR

....

....

....

....

....

....

SOMETHING I WANT US TO DO
TOGETHER IN THE NEXT YEAR

....

....

....

FROM ME TO YOU...

CHECK THE
BACK POCKET

2

THRILLING AT 3

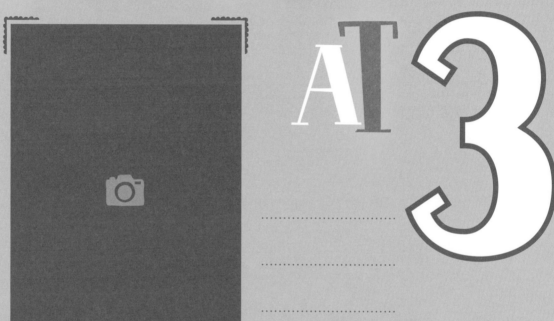

AS YOU EXPLORE YOUR EVER-EXPANDING WORLD,
YOU STILL ENJOY THESE FAVORITE PLACES.

SUCH A GOOD HELPER

WAYS YOU LIKE TO HELP YOUR FAMILY

....

....

WAYS YOU LIKE TO HELP
YOUR FRIENDS

....

....

....

....

....

....

SKILLS THAT STILL NEED JUST A LITTLE MORE PRACTICE

....

....

LiTTLE INVESTiGATOR

YOUR FAVORITE QUESTION TO ASK IS

....

FUNNY OBSERVATIONS YOU'VE MADE

....

....

YOU LIKE TO PRETEND BY

....

....

IN THIS PHOTO,
YOU'RE PRETENDING TO ➜

....

WITH ....

....

ALL ABOUT FEELINGS

YOU ARE AFRAID OF ...., BUT YOU ARE

VERY BRAVE WHEN IT COMES TO ....

.... ALWAYS BRINGS A SMILE TO YOUR FACE.

THIS IS WHAT YOUR BIGGEST SMILE LOOKS LIKE.

YOU'RE EAGER TO LEARN ABOUT

....

BIRTHDAY FUN

WE CELEBRATED YOUR THIRD BIRTHDAY WITH

THEME ....

GUESTS ....

ACTIVITIES ....

THE HIGHLIGHT OF THE CELEBRATION WAS

....

LAUGHTER *and* LOVE

I CAN'T HELP BUT LAUGH WHEN YOU

....

SOMETHING YOU DO
THAT WARMS MY HEART

....

....

FROM ME TO YOU...

CHECK THE
BACK POCKET

3

FABULOUS AT 4

NEW GIFTS WITHIN YOU EMERGE ALL THE TIME!
HERE YOU ARE DOING SOMETHING YOU LOVE.

YOUR FAVORITES RIGHT NOW

TOYS AND GAMES ....

....

....

PLAYMATES ....

....

COLOR ....

FOOD ....

SHOWS AND MOVIES ....

....

....

BOOKS ....

....

TOPIC TO TALK ABOUT ....

....

....

DEVELOPING ARTIST

YOUR FAVORITE THING TO DRAW OR COLOR IS

....

....

HERE IS SOME OF YOUR ART

WHAT YOU TOLD ME ABOUT THIS ARTWORK

....

....

LOOKING INTO THE FUTURE

WHAT YOU SAY YOU WANT TO BE WHEN YOU GROW UP

....

....

WHAT YOU THINK THE WORLD WILL BE LIKE WHEN YOU'RE 100

....

....

....

....

YEARS FROM NOW, I CAN IMAGINE YOU

....

....

....

....

4

BIRTHDAY FUN

WE CELEBRATED YOUR FOURTH BIRTHDAY WITH

THEME ....

GUESTS ....

ACTIVITIES ....

THE HIGHLIGHT OF THE CELEBRATION WAS

....

GROWING IN SO MANY WAYS

A TIME I WAS REALLY PROUD OF YOU IN THE PAST YEAR

....

....

....

....

....

....

I CAN'T WAIT TO DO THIS
WITH YOU IN THE NEXT YEAR

....

....

....

FROM ME TO YOU...

CHECK THE
BACK POCKET

4

SHINING AT 5

YOU LIGHT UP MY WORLD! HERE IS A PICTURE OF
YOU THAT MAKES ME SMILE—AND WHY.

TALENT SHOW

TALENTS YOU ENJOY
SHARING WITH OTHERS

....

....

....

....

....

....

....

A HIDDEN TALENT I SEE IN YOU THAT YOU HAVEN'T REALIZED YET

....

SOMETHING NEW YOU'RE LEARNING RIGHT NOW

....

....

YOU DOING YOU

YOUR FAVORITE ACTIVITY WHEN YOU'RE WITH FRIENDS

....

YOUR FAVORITE ACTIVITY WHEN YOU'RE WITH FAMILY

....

YOUR FAVORITE ACTIVITY DURING INDEPENDENT TIME

....

A DEEPER DIVE

YOU GET EXCITED WHEN ....

YOU GET FRUSTRATED WHEN ....

WAYS IN WHICH YOU ARE A LOT LIKE ME

....

....

....

....

WAYS IN WHICH WE ARE VERY DIFFERENT

....

....

....

....

....

5

BiRTHDAY FUN

WE CELEBRATED YOUR FIFTH BIRTHDAY WITH

THEME ....

GUESTS ....

ACTIVITIES ....

THE HIGHLIGHT OF THE CELEBRATION WAS

....

LOOKING BACK

IF I COULD RELIVE ONE MOMENT
WITH YOU FROM THE PAST YEAR,
IT WOULD BE

....

....

....

....

....

THE BEST GIFT YOU'VE GIVEN ME

....

....

....

FROM ME TO YOU...

CHECK THE
BACK POCKET

5

SUPER AT 6

SO MANY LITTLE THINGS ABOUT YOU AMAZE ME EVERY DAY. IF I COULD GIVE YOU A SUPERHERO NAME, IT WOULD BE ....

YOUR FANTASTIC FEATS

HERE ARE SIX ACCOMPLISHMENTS (BIG OR LITTLE) FROM THE PAST YEAR

1. ....
2. ....
3. ....
4. ....
5. ....
6. ....

JUST IMAGINE

IF YOU COULD EAT ONLY ONE FOOD, IT WOULD BE

....

IF YOU HAD A THEME SONG, IT WOULD BE

....

IF YOU COULD REDECORATE YOUR ROOM ANY WAY YOU WANT,
IT WOULD LOOK LIKE

....

....

IF YOU COULD SPEND A DAY WITH SOMEONE FAMOUS,
YOU WOULD CHOOSE

....

IF YOU COULD HAVE ANY JOB WHEN YOU GROW UP,
YOU WOULD WANT TO

....

PEOPLE AND PLACES

PEOPLE YOU LOVE TO
SPEND TIME WITH

....

....

....

....

....

PLACES YOU LOVE TO GO

....

PLACES YOU *DON'T* LIKE TO GO

....

....

BiRTHDAY FUN

WE CELEBRATED YOUR SIXTH BIRTHDAY WITH

THEME ....

GUESTS ....

ACTIVITIES ....

THE HIGHLIGHT OF THE CELEBRATION WAS

....

COMPARING MEMORIES

WHAT YOU CAN RECALL AS YOUR EARLIEST MEMORY

....

....

....

....

AN EARLY MEMORY OF YOU
THAT I TREASURE

....

....

....

FROM ME TO YOU...

CHECK THE
BACK POCKET

6

SENSATIONAL AT 7

....
....
....
....

YOU'RE LEARNING SO MUCH!
YOUR FAVORITE PARTS OF SCHOOL ARE...

PEEK INSIDE

THIS IS YOU WITH YOUR SCHOOL BAG

↓

YOU CHOSE IT BECAUSE

....

IF YOU COULD SNEAK YOUR FAVORITE THINGS INSIDE,
I WOULD PROBABLY FIND

....

SCHOOL DAYS

MOST DAYS, YOUR LUNCH IS

....

HOW YOU TRAVEL TO AND FROM SCHOOL

....

....

YOUR FAVORITE CLASSMATES

....

....

....

....

....

....

....

ALL ABOUT ACTIVITIES

YOUR FAVORITE ORGANIZED ACTIVITY IS

....

....

YOUR FAVORITE FREE TIME ACTIVITY IS

....

....

BIRTHDAY FUN

WE CELEBRATED YOUR SEVENTH BIRTHDAY WITH

THEME ....

GUESTS ....

ACTIVITIES ....

THE HIGHLIGHT OF THE CELEBRATION WAS

....

WISHES AND HOPES

WHAT I WISH I COULD FREEZE ABOUT YOUR AGE RIGHT NOW

....

....

....

....

WHAT I HOPE YOU'VE LEARNED
IN THE PAST YEAR

....

....

....

FROM ME TO YOU...

CHECK THE
BACK POCKET

7

AWESOME AT 8

TO INTRODUCE YOU TO SOMEONE,
I WOULD USE THIS PHOTO AND THESE THREE WORDS.

WHAT MAKES YOU SMILE

ACTIVITIES ....

....

....

FOOD ....

....

FRIENDS ....

....

PLACES ....

....

BOOKS ....

....

MUSIC ....

....

SHOWS AND MOVIES ....

....

8

ALL ABOUT FEELINGS

YOU ARE AFRAID OF ...., BUT YOU ARE

VERY BRAVE WHEN IT COMES TO ....

YOU'RE EAGER TO LEARN ABOUT

....

....

HOW I CAN
MAKE YOU LAUGH

....

....

....

....

....

....

LOOKING INTO THE FUTURE

WHAT YOU CAN'T WAIT TO GET OLD ENOUGH TO DO

....

....

....

WHAT YOU SAY YOU WANT TO BE WHEN YOU GROW UP

....

....

YEARS FROM NOW, I CAN IMAGINE YOU

....

....

....

....

8

BIRTHDAY FUN

WE CELEBRATED YOUR EIGHTH BIRTHDAY WITH

THEME ....

GUESTS ....

ACTIVITIES ....

THE HIGHLIGHT OF THE CELEBRATION WAS

....

YOU SHOULD KNOW

YOU HAVE A SPECIAL TALENT FOR

....

....

....

....

....

....

....

I'M PROUD OF YOU FOR

....

....

....

FROM ME TO YOU...

CHECK THE
BACK POCKET

8

DYNAMITE AT 9

....

....

....

IT'S FUN TO WATCH YOUR INTERESTS DEVELOP.
LOOK AT HOW EXCITED YOU ARE TO...

A DAY IN YOUR LIFE

WHAT A TYPICAL WEEKDAY LOOKS LIKE FOR YOU

....

....

....

....

WHAT A TYPICAL WEEKEND LOOKS LIKE FOR YOU

....

....

....

....

TIMES I SEE YOU REALLY COME ALIVE

....

....

....

9

THIS IS YOU

WHAT MAKES YOU LAUGH ....

....

PEOPLE YOU SPEND THE MOST TIME WITH ....

....

📷

WHAT YOU LOVE TO WEAR ....

....

JUST IMAGINE

IF YOU COULD WIN A SHOPPING SPREE AT ANY STORE,
YOU WOULD WANT IT TO BE

....

IF YOU COULD CHOOSE A VACATION DESTINATION, IT WOULD BE

....

IF YOU COULD APPEAR ON ANY TV SHOW, IT WOULD BE

....

IF YOU COULD SPEND A DAY WITH SOMEONE FAMOUS,
YOU WOULD CHOOSE

....

IF YOU COULD HAVE ANY JOB WHEN YOU GROW UP,
YOU WOULD WANT TO

....

....

9

BIRTHDAY FUN

WE CELEBRATED YOUR NINTH BIRTHDAY WITH

THEME ....

GUESTS ....

ACTIVITIES ....

THE HIGHLIGHT OF THE CELEBRATION WAS

....

ALL IN THE FAMILY

AT THIS AGE, YOU LOOK VERY MUCH LIKE

YOUR PERSONALITY REMINDS ME MOST OF

FROM ME TO YOU...

CHECK THE BACK POCKET

9

TOPS AT 10

YOU'RE GROWING IN SO MANY WAYS!
I MOST APPRECIATE YOUR STRIDES
IN THIS AREA IN THE PAST YEAR.

YOUR FAVORITES RIGHT NOW

ACTIVITIES ....

....

....

ENTERTAINMENT ....

....

....

FRIENDS ....

....

....

SCHOOL SUBJECT ....

COLOR ....

FOOD ....

TOPIC TO TALK ABOUT ....

....

....

10

LAUGHTER AND LOVE

I CAN'T HELP BUT LAUGH WHEN YOU ....

TO MAKE YOU LAUGH, I CAN ....

HOW WE ENJOY SPENDING TIME TOGETHER

....

....

YOU SHOULD KNOW

A HIDDEN TALENT I SEE IN YOU THAT YOU HAVEN'T REALIZED YET

....

....

....

A TIME I WAS REALLY PROUD OF YOU IN THE PAST YEAR

....

....

....

I CAN'T WAIT TO DO THIS WITH YOU IN THE NEXT YEAR

....

....

....

....

10

BIRTHDAY FUN

WE CELEBRATED YOUR TENTH BIRTHDAY WITH

THEME

GUESTS

ACTIVITIES

THE HIGHLIGHT OF THE CELEBRATION WAS

CELEBRATING YOU

THIS PHOTO TOTALLY CAPTURES YOU BEING YOU!

📷

THREE WORDS THAT
DESCRIBE YOU

....

....

....

FROM ME TO YOU...

CHECK THE
BACK POCKET

10

EXCELLENT AT 11

THE TIME WE SPEND TOGETHER IS SPECIAL. ONE OF MY FAVORITE MEMORIES FROM THE PAST YEAR IS...

NEW DiSCOVERIES THiS YEAR

NEW PLACES YOU WENT

....

....

....

....

....

....

....

NEW PEOPLE YOU MET

....

....

NEW SKILLS/INFORMATION YOU LEARNED

....

....

11

THIS IS YOU

YOU GET EXCITED WHEN ....
....

YOU GET FRUSTRATED WHEN ....
....

📷

YOUR PERFECT DAY WOULD BE ....
....

LOOKING INTO THE FUTURE

WHAT YOU SAY YOU WANT TO BE WHEN YOU GROW UP

....

....

WHAT YOU THINK THE WORLD WILL BE LIKE WHEN YOU'RE 100

....

....

....

....

I CAN'T WAIT TO DO THIS WITH YOU IN THE NEXT YEAR

....

....

....

....

11

BIRTHDAY FUN

WE CELEBRATED YOUR ELEVENTH BIRTHDAY WITH

THEME ....

GUESTS ....

ACTIVITIES ....

THE HIGHLIGHT OF THE CELEBRATION WAS

....

BETWEEN YOU AND ME

WAYS IN WHICH YOU ARE A LOT LIKE ME

....

....

....

....

WAYS IN WHICH WE ARE
VERY DIFFERENT

....

....

....

FROM ME TO YOU...

CHECK THE
BACK POCKET

11

TALENTED AT 12

YOUR SMILE SHINES THE BRIGHTEST
WHEN YOU ARE...

YOU DOING YOU

YOUR FAVORITE ACTIVITY WHEN YOU'RE WITH FRIENDS

....

....

YOUR FAVORITE ACTIVITY
WHEN YOU'RE WITH FAMILY

....

....

....

....

....

YOUR FAVORITE ACTIVITY DURING INDEPENDENT TIME

....

....

TALENT SHOW

TALENTS YOU ENJOY
SHARING WITH OTHERS

....

....

....

....

....

....

A HIDDEN TALENT I SEE IN YOU THAT YOU HAVEN'T REALIZED YET

....

....

SOMETHING NEW YOU'RE LEARNING RIGHT NOW

....

....

SPECIAL GIFTS FROM YOU

SOMETHING I HAVE LEARNED
FROM YOU IN THE PAST YEAR

....

....

....

....

....

....

....

HOW YOU SHOW YOUR LOVE FOR FRIENDS AND FAMILY

....

....

....

....

12

BIRTHDAY FUN

WE CELEBRATED YOUR TWELFTH BIRTHDAY WITH

THEME ....

GUESTS ....

ACTIVITIES ....

THE HIGHLIGHT OF THE CELEBRATION WAS

....

LET'S TALK

SOME OF THE STRANGEST TOPICS WE TALK ABOUT

....

....

....

....

....

....

SERIOUS CONVERSATIONS WE'VE HAD

....

....

FROM ME TO YOU...

CHECK THE BACK POCKET

12

SUPREME AT 13

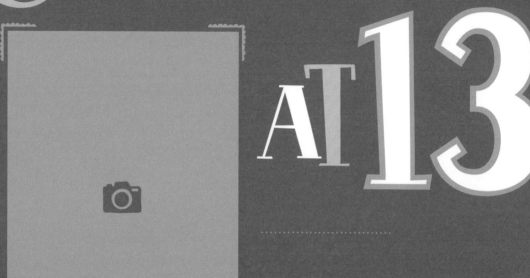

WHEN I LOOK AT THIS PICTURE
OF YOU FROM THE PAST YEAR, I SEE...

IN-BETWEEN DAYS

WAYS IN WHICH I SEE YOU GROWING UP

....

....

....

....

WAYS THAT YOU'RE STILL HOLDING ON TO PARTS OF YOUR CHILDHOOD

....

....

....

....

TRADITIONS I HOPE WE CONTINUE

....

....

....

13

ALL ABOUT FEELINGS

YOU ARE AFRAID OF ...., BUT YOU ARE

VERY BRAVE WHEN IT COMES TO ....

YOU'RE EAGER TO

....

....

HOW I CAN MAKE YOU LAUGH

....

....

....

....

....

....

....

A DAY IN YOUR LIFE

WHAT A TYPICAL WEEKDAY LOOKS LIKE FOR YOU

....

....

....

....

WHAT A TYPICAL WEEKEND LOOKS LIKE FOR YOU

....

....

....

....

TIMES I SEE YOU REALLY COME ALIVE

....

....

....

13

BiRTHDAY FUN

WE CELEBRATED YOUR THIRTEENTH BIRTHDAY WITH

THEME ....

GUESTS ....

ACTIVITIES ....

THE HIGHLIGHT OF THE CELEBRATION WAS

....

WISHES AND HOPES

WHAT I WISH I COULD FREEZE
ABOUT YOUR AGE RIGHT NOW

....

....

....

....

....

....

WHAT I HOPE YOU'VE LEARNED
IN THE PAST YEAR

....

....

....

....

FROM ME TO YOU...

CHECK THE
BACK POCKET

13

PHENOMENAL AT 14

YOU ARE UNIQUELY YOU!
THIS PHOTO OF YOU IS ALL THE EVIDENCE NEEDED.

YOUR FAVORITES RIGHT NOW

ACTIVITIES ....

....

....

ENTERTAINMENT ....

....

....

FRIENDS ....

....

....

SCHOOL SUBJECT ....

COLOR ....

FOOD ....

TOPIC TO TALK ABOUT ....

....

....

14

CELEBRATING YOU

THREE WORDS THAT
DESCRIBE YOU

....

....

....

....

....

THE AFFECTIONATE NICKNAMES WE CALL YOU

....

....

....

IF YOU HAD A THEME SONG, IT WOULD BE

....

YOU SHOULD KNOW

SOMETHING AMAZING I SEE DEVELOPING IN YOU

....

....

....

A TIME I WAS REALLY PROUD OF YOU IN THE PAST YEAR

....

....

....

I CAN'T WAIT TO DO THIS WITH YOU IN THE NEXT YEAR

....

....

....

14

BIRTHDAY FUN

WE CELEBRATED YOUR FOURTEENTH BIRTHDAY WITH

THEME ....

GUESTS ....

ACTIVITIES ....

THE HIGHLIGHT OF THE CELEBRATION WAS

....

LOOKING INTO THE FUTURE

WHAT YOU CAN'T WAIT TO GET OLDER TO DO

....

....

....

....

YEARS FROM NOW,
I CAN IMAGINE YOU

....

....

....

FROM ME TO YOU...

CHECK THE
BACK POCKET

14

FANTASTIC AT 15

THESE ARE THE THREE PLACES
YOU'RE LIKELY TO BE THESE DAYS.
HERE YOU ARE IN ONE OF YOUR HAPPY PLACES!

JUST IMAGINE

IF YOU COULD WIN A SHOPPING SPREE AT ANY STORE,
YOU WOULD WANT IT TO BE

....

IF YOU COULD CHOOSE A VACATION DESTINATION, IT WOULD BE

....

IF YOU COULD APPEAR ON ANY TV SHOW, IT WOULD BE

....

IF YOU COULD SPEND A DAY WITH SOMEONE FAMOUS,
YOU WOULD CHOOSE

....

IF YOU COULD HAVE ANY JOB WHEN YOU GROW UP,
YOU WOULD WANT TO

....

....

THIS IS YOU

WHAT MAKES YOU LAUGH ....

....

PEOPLE YOU SPEND THE MOST TIME WITH ....

....

WHAT YOU LOVE TO WEAR ....

....

ALL IN THE FAMILY

AT THIS AGE, YOU LOOK VERY MUCH LIKE ....

YOUR PERSONALITY REMINDS ME MOST OF

....

HOW I WOULD DESCRIBE YOUR ROLE IN OUR FAMILY

....

BIRTHDAY FUN

WE CELEBRATED YOUR FIFTEENTH BIRTHDAY WITH

THEME ....

GUESTS ....

ACTIVITIES ....

THE HIGHLIGHT OF THE CELEBRATION WAS

....

LAUGHTER AND LOVE

HOW YOU MAKE ME LAUGH

....

....

....

....

....

....

HOW WE SHOW OUR LOVE

FOR EACH OTHER

....

....

....

....

FROM ME TO YOU...

CHECK THE BACK POCKET

15

SPECIAL

AT 16

WHEN I LOOK AT YOU NOW, I REMEMBER THIS
FROM WHEN YOU WERE YOUNGER.

YOUR FANTASTIC FEATS

HERE ARE SIX ACCOMPLISHMENTS (BIG OR LITTLE) FROM THE PAST YEAR

1. ....

2. ....

3. ....

4. ....

5. ....

6. ....

16

ALL ABOUT ACTIVITIES

YOUR FAVORITE
ORGANIZED ACTIVITY IS

....

....

....

....

....

....

....

YOUR FAVORITE FREE TIME ACTIVITY IS

....

....

....

....

WISHES AND HOPES

WHAT I WISH I COULD FREEZE ABOUT YOUR AGE RIGHT NOW

....

....

....

WHAT I HOPE YOU'VE LEARNED IN THE PAST YEAR

....

....

....

YEARS FROM NOW, I CAN IMAGINE YOU

....

....

....

....

16

BIRTHDAY FUN

WE CELEBRATED YOUR SIXTEENTH BIRTHDAY WITH

THEME ....

GUESTS ....

ACTIVITIES ....

THE HIGHLIGHT OF THE CELEBRATION WAS

....

YOU MAKE ME SMILE

ONE WAY YOU'VE SURPRISED ME IN THE PAST YEAR

....

....

....

....

I'M PROUD OF YOU FOR

....

....

....

....

FROM ME TO YOU...

CHECK THE BACK POCKET

16

STELLAR AT 17

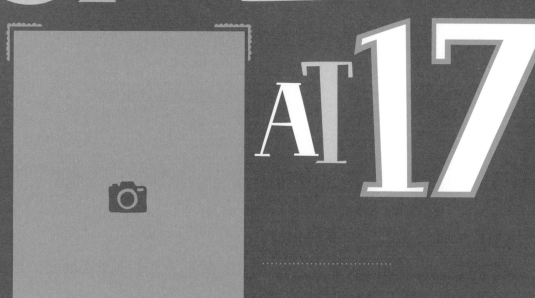

THIS PHOTO OF YOU BRINGS TO MIND
THESE THREE WORDS...

A DAY IN YOUR LIFE

WHAT A TYPICAL WEEKDAY LOOKS LIKE FOR YOU

....

....

....

....

WHAT A TYPICAL WEEKEND LOOKS LIKE FOR YOU

....

....

....

....

TIMES I SEE YOU REALLY COME ALIVE

....

....

....

17

ALL ABOUT FEELINGS

YOU ARE AFRAID OF ...., BUT YOU ARE

VERY BRAVE WHEN IT COMES TO ....

YOU'RE EAGER TO

....

....

.... ALWAYS BRINGS A SMILE TO YOUR FACE.

LOOKING INTO THE FUTURE

WHERE YOU SAY YOU'LL BE IN 10 YEARS

....

....

....

....

WHERE I THINK YOU'LL BE IN 10 YEARS

....

....

....

I CAN'T WAIT TO DO THIS WITH YOU IN THE NEXT YEAR

....

....

....

....

17

BIRTHDAY FUN

WE CELEBRATED YOUR SEVENTEENTH BIRTHDAY WITH

THEME ....

GUESTS ....

ACTIVITIES ....

THE HIGHLIGHT OF THE CELEBRATION WAS

....

LET'S TALK

SOME OF THE STRANGEST TOPICS WE TALK ABOUT

....

....

....

....

....

....

SERIOUS CONVERSATIONS WE'VE HAD

....

....

....

....

....

....

FROM ME TO YOU...

CHECK THE
BACK POCKET

17

AMAZING AT 18

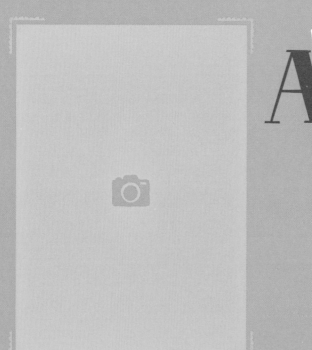

YOU CONTINUE TO LIGHT UP MY WORLD.
HERE YOU ARE LIGHTING UP THE GREATER WORLD BY...

YOUR FAVORITES RIGHT NOW

ACTIVITIES ....

....

....

ENTERTAINMENT ....

....

....

FRIENDS ....

....

....

SCHOOL SUBJECT ....

COLOR ....

FOOD ....

TOPIC TO TALK ABOUT ....

....

....

18

GROWING IN SO MANY WAYS

IN THESE WAYS, I STILL SEE THAT
TODDLER I WROTE ABOUT IN THE
BEGINNING OF THIS JOURNAL

....

....

....

....

....

....

AT THE SAME TIME, YOU'VE GROWN IN THESE WAYS
I COULDN'T HAVE PREDICTED

....

....

....

SPECIAL GIFTS FROM YOU

SOMETHING I HAVE LEARNED
FROM YOU IN THE PAST YEAR

....

....

....

....

....

....

HOW YOU SHOW YOUR LOVE FOR FRIENDS AND FAMILY

....

....

....

....

....

18

BIRTHDAY FUN

WE CELEBRATED YOUR EIGHTEENTH BIRTHDAY WITH

THEME ....

GUESTS ....

ACTIVITIES ....

THE HIGHLIGHT OF THE CELEBRATION WAS

....

YOU SHOULD KNOW

A TIME I WAS REALLY PROUD
OF YOU IN THE PAST YEAR

....

....

....

....

....

SOMETHING I CAN'T WAIT TO SEE YOU DO ON YOUR OWN

....

....

....

....

FROM ME TO YOU...

CHECK THE
BACK POCKET

18

LOVE LETTERS

EACH YEAR, I'VE TUCKED A LITTLE MORE OBSERVATION,
ADVICE, AND LOVE FOR YOU INTO THE BACK OF THIS BOOK.

JUST FLIP THE PAGE TO FIND...

THE LETTERS
WAITING FOR
YOU

AS YOU READ THE YEARS' JOURNAL ENTRIES,
FIND THE LETTER WITH THE MATCHING AGE LABELED
ON THE OUTSIDE TO CONTINUE THE STORY.